TILLS™

TEST OF INTEGRATED LANGUAGE & LITERACY SKILLS™

Examiner Record Form

CALCULATION OF STUDENT'S AGE		
Test date		
Year:_____	Month:_____	Day:_____
Birth date		
Year:_____	Month:_____	Day:_____
Age at test		
Year:_____	Month:_____	Day:_____

Student name: ______________________________ Grade: ________ School: ________________________

Scoring Chart

Examiner name: ______________________________

Step 1: Enter raw scores for all subtests administered.

Step 2: Look up the Subtest Standard Scores and Percentile Ranks for the student's age in the *Examiner's Manual* Appendix and enter them in the Subtest Scores section.

Step 3: Copy the Standard Scores into the open white cells on the same rows in the Composite of Subtest Standard Scores section.

Step 4: Copy the Standard Scores into the open white cells in the same rows in the age-appropriate column in the Identification Core Scores section.

Step 5: Enter the Sum of the Subtest Standard Scores in all columns where all subtests have been administered.

Step 6: Look up the Sums of Subtest Standard Scores for the student's age in the *Examiner's Manual* Appendix to find the Standard Scores and Percentile Ranks.

	Subtest Scores and TILLS Total			Composite of Subtest Standard Scores				Identification Core Scores		
Subtest	Raw Score	Standard Score and TILLS Total	Percentile Rank	Sound/Word Composite Score	Sentence/Discourse Composite Score	Oral Composite Score	Written Composite Score	Identification Core for 6- to 7-year-olds	Identification Core for 8- to 11-year-olds	Identification Core for 12- to 18-year-olds
1 VA										
2 PA										
3 SR										
4 NWRep										
5 NWSpell*										
6 LC										
7 RC*										
8 FD										
9 DSR										
10 NWRead*										
11 RF*										
12a WE-Disc*										
12b WE-Sent*										
12c WE-Word*										
13 SC										
14 DSF										
15 DSB										
Sum of the Subtest Standard Scores										
Standard Scores of the TILLS Total and Composites										
Percentile Ranks for the TILLS Total and Composites										

*Note: For children 6;0–6;5, do not administer the NWSpell, RC, NWRead, RF, and WE subtests.

Key for Subtests: VA = Vocabulary Awareness, PA = Phonemic Awareness, SR = Story Retelling, NWRep = Nonword Repetition, NWSpell = Nonword Spelling, LC = Listening Comprehension, RC = Reading Comprehension, FD = Following Directions, DSR = Delayed Story Retelling, NWRead = Nonword Reading, RF = Reading Fluency, WE-Disc = Written Expression–Discourse Score, WE-Sent = Written Expression–Sentence Score, WE-Word = Written Expression–Word Score, SC = Social Communication, DSF=Digit Span Forward, DSB = Digit Span Backward.

SUBTEST 1: Vocabulary Awareness (VA)

Average time to administer: 15 minutes

Materials: *Stimulus Book* (pp. 3–55)

Start rule: ➡ Start points for age ranges are indicated by arrows

Repetition: Allowed

Basal rule: 4 consecutive scores of 2 (both parts of each item must be correct)

Ceiling rule: 6 scores of 0 within a sequence of 8 consecutive items (both parts of each item must be incorrect on 6 out of 8 items)

Directions

- Open the *Stimulus Book* to page 3. Say, ***"Here are three words. Let's read them together."*** The examiner reads all stimuli on this subtest. Students are not required to read along. ***"dog–cat–bone"***
- Say, ***"Tell me two words that go together."*** Then ask, ***"Why?"***
- Coaching is allowed for practice items: If the student's response to "Why?" on either practice item is not a good/primary/dominant reason, say, ***"Can you think of a better reason to put dog and cat*** [or dog and bone] ***together?"*** If the student still does not give an appropriate answer, probe, ***"Do you think they are both animals*** [or dogs like bones]***? How about that for a reason? Now can you tell me two other words that go together in a different way?"*** Then ask, ***"Why?"*** (Coach for a reason if necessary.)
- Proceed to the second practice item, ***light–sun–feather,*** and coach as necessary to point out that some words have more than one meaning. Say, ***"Any questions?"*** (Answer.)
- ***"Okay. Let's begin."*** Show the first test item. Read the three words aloud with or for the student. Circle the printed reason if given, or record the response if the student says something else.
- As needed, say, ***"What other two are you putting together?"*** and ***"Why?"*** (Be sure to ask for two pairs per item.) Continue reading aloud for all items.

Probes Probe for more elaborate answers only if the student says the words "mean the same thing." Ask, ***"Can you tell me what they mean?"*** If the student refers to spelling, coach him/her to focus on meaning rather than what the words look like. If the student gives a meaning that applies to all three words, probe for how the two chosen words go together in a way that the third one does not. Otherwise, just ask for pairings and rationale (no further probing about meaning is allowed), and record the student's initial response. If the student revises spontaneously, score the revised response, making note of the initial response. If a student asks what a word means, say, ***"I can't tell you"*** and write DK (for "don't know"). A general prompt also may be used to tell the student that it is okay to guess or say, "I don't know."

Recording & Scoring

- Circle the response pairs the student gives in separate columns. The order of pairs does not matter.
- For each pair, underline the student's reason, or write in a reason that is not listed.
- **Score 1** for each correct word pair and reason (must get both pair and reason correct to score).
- **Score 0** for each incorrect word pair and/or reason or if the student says, "I don't know that word."
- Record the total score (0–2) for each item pair (a + b) in the Total Item Score column on the right.
- Add the points in the right-hand column to yield the total subtest score.

Practice Items

dog–cat–bone	**dog**–cat–**bone**
Both animals / pets	Dogs like / eat / chew / bury bones
light–sun–feather	**light**–sun–**feather**
Sun gives light / both bright	Feather is light / not heavy

Subtest Items

Total Item Score (a + b)

Start	Item			Item			Total Item Score (a + b)
6–11 ➡	1a. **pen**–pig–**paper**	0	1	1b. **pen–pig**–paper	0	1	
	Use pen to write on paper			Keep a pig in a pen			
	2a. **thorn–rose**–daisy	0	1	2b. thorn–**rose–daisy**	0	1	
	Roses have thorns			Both flowers			
	3a. **kite–airplane**–train	0	1	3b. kite–**airplane–train**	0	1	
	Both fly / go in sky (*not* a kite can be shaped like an airplane)			Both transportation / carry people / can ride in them Both have wheels / engines / use electricity / are machines (*not* you can take airplanes on a train)			

(continued)

	Item a			Item b			**Total Item Score (a + b)**
	4a. **saw–hammer**–eyes	0	1	4b. **saw**–hammer–**eyes**	0	1	
	Both tools / have handles			Eyes for seeing / I saw with my eyes			
12–13	5a. **bark–growl**–tree	0	1	5b. **bark**–growl–**tree**	0	1	
	Both sounds a dog makes			Bark covers / grows on tree			
	6a. **taste**–nose–**smell**	0	1	6b. taste–**nose–smell**	0	1	
	Both senses (*not* you can smell and taste food)			Smell with nose / use nose to smell			
14+	7a. **oven**–ice cream–**freezer**	0	1	7b. oven–**ice cream–freezer**	0	1	
	Both appliances / make food hot or cold (*not* in the kitchen)			Ice cream goes in freezer			
	8a. **painter**–elevator–**ladder**	0	1	8b. painter–**elevator–ladder**	0	1	
	Painter uses / stands on ladder / paints with a ladder / needs a ladder to paint			Use to go up / reach high places			
	9a. **stomach–swallow**–cardinal	0	1	9b. stomach–**swallow–cardinal**	0	1	
	When swallowed, food goes to stomach			Both birds			
	10a. **sphinx–pyramid**–triangle	0	1	10b. sphinx–**pyramid–triangle**	0	1	
	Both found in Egypt / in desert Both ancient			Pyramid is shaped like triangle Both shapes			
	11a. **left**–correct–**right**	0	1	11b. left–**correct–right**	0	1	
	Tell opposite directions (or gestures to show)			Both describe picking a good answer / making a good choice			
	12a. **diamond–baseball**–ruby	0	1	12b. **diamond**–baseball–**ruby**	0	1	
	Play baseball on a diamond / baseball field called diamond			Both jewels / rocks / gems / minerals Both shiny / expensive / come from mines			
	13a. **bat–owl**–eagle	0	1	13b. bat–**owl–eagle**	0	1	
	Nocturnal, up at night (*not* predators)			Both birds / have feathers / have beaks / have talons / make nests (*not* predators)			
	14a. **hammer–hatchet**–tree	0	1	14b. hammer–**hatchet–tree**	0	1	
	Both tools / have handles			Use hatchet to cut down tree			
	15a. **knee–foot**–elbow	0	1	15b. **knee**–foot–**elbow**	0	1	
	Both on leg / used to walk			Both bend / are joints (*not* have round knobs or are hard)			
	16a. **fan–propeller**–admirer	0	1	16b. **fan**–propeller–**admirer**	0	1	
	Both have blades / go around / move air A fan has a propeller (can gesture spinning)			Both mean to like something / someone			

(continued)

Item a			Item b			**Total Item Score (a + b)**
17a. **march–step**–stair	0	1	17b. march–**step–stair**	0	1	
Marching is a / uses a special kind of step / stepping in rhythm			Both parts of a staircase / for going up or down a level in a building / step is part of a stair (*not* you can step upstairs; must get noun meaning)			
18a. **scales–ounce**–thermometer	0	1	18b. **scales**–ounce–**thermometer**	0	1	
Both are related to weight / weigh ounces with a scale			Both used to measure / thermometer has a scale / in a doctor's office			
19a. **canary–banana**–hawk	0	1	19b. **canary**–banana–**hawk**	0	1	
Both yellow / found in tropics (*not* canaries eat bananas)			Both birds			
20a. **capsule**–pill–**spaceship**	0	1	20b. **capsule–pill**–spaceship	0	1	
Both used for space travel / capsule is part of spaceship / astronaut rides in the capsule			Both medicine you swallow / pill can take form of capsule / pills are in capsules			
21a. **trout–flounder**–struggle	0	1	21b. trout–**flounder–struggle**	0	1	
Both fish			Both mean having trouble / difficulty with something			
22a. **plum**–cut–**prune**	0	1	22b. plum–**cut–prune**	0	1	
Both fruit / prune is a dried plum			Both mean to use something sharp to slice / cut (*not* you can cut a prune or plum)			
23a. **conceal–hide**–skin	0	1	23b. conceal–**hide–skin**	0	1	
Both mean to keep out of sight Conceal means you're going to hide something (*not* your skin conceals your bones)			Both cover body / animals (*not* you use concealer on your skin)			
24a. **mean–average**–spite	0	1	24b. **mean**–average–**spite**	0	1	
Both terms for computing a number / telling the middle number / used in math			Both describe person who is not nice / tries to get back at someone			
25a. **nylon–plastic**–cotton	0	1	25b. **nylon**–plastic–**cotton**	0	1	
Both synthetic / manmade / made from petroleum			Both types of fabric / used for clothing			

Total score: _____ / 50

Qualitative observations:

SUBTEST 2: Phonemic Awareness (PA)

Average time to administer: 3 minutes
Materials: Audio recording device (recommended)
Start rule: ➡ Start points for age ranges are indicated by arrows
Repetition: No (unless ambient noise interferes)
Basal rule: 6 consecutive scores of 1
Ceiling rule: Scores 0 on 6 out of 8 consecutive items

Directions

- Begin recording.
- Say, ***"I am going to say a pretend word that is not a real word. Your job is to say the word back to me, but without the first sound. Let's practice." "If the word is bip, and we take away the first sound, bip becomes*** [hesitate, encourage choral response]...***ip." "If the word is stig, and we take away the first sound, stig becomes...tig."***
- Reinforce practice items as appropriate. Provide coaching if necessary to remove only the first sound on "stig."
- Say, ***"Any questions?"*** (Answer.) ***"Let's begin."*** Use the pattern "[test item] becomes [student response]."

Probes Use hesitating and coaching as needed only during practice. For test items, do **not** remind the student to remove only the first sound if the student reverts to a pattern of removing the full consonant cluster during testing.

Recording & Scoring

- **Score 1** if the student accurately produces all (and only) the remaining sounds in the word (after removing only the initial phoneme). If the student is unable to perform the task with the practice items even after additional coaching, administer the test items starting with Item 1 regardless of the student's age and test until the ceiling is reached.
- **Score 0** if the response does not match the expected response, and *record the student's exact response* using either traditional orthography (alphabetic letters) or phonetic transcription or mark changes on the expected response.
- **IMPORTANT:** If the student uses a consistent pattern of misarticulation or regional vowel pronunciation in spontaneous speaking (e.g., th/s, w/l, w/r), do not penalize the substituted sounds.

Practice Items

Item	Phonetic spelling	Spoken response
bip → ip	/bɪp/ → /ɪp/	
stig → tig	/stɪg/ → /tɪg/	

Subtest Items

Start	Item	Phonetic spelling	Spoken response	Score	
6–7	1. dop → op	/dap / →/ap /		0	1
	2. bap → ap	/bæp / → /æp /		0	1
	3. blom → lom	/blam/ → /lam/		0	1
	4. molk → olk	/molk/ → /olk/		0	1
	5. gilf → ilf	/gɪlf/ → /ɪlf/		0	1
	6. flig → lig	/flɪg / → /lɪg /		0	1
	7. lekel → ekel	/lɛkəl/ → /ɛkəl/		0	1
8–14	8. krit → rit	/krɪt/ → /rɪt/		0	1
	9. swog → wog	/swɔg / →/wɔg /		0	1
	10. treeg → reeg	/trig/ →/rig/		0	1
15+	11. brogger → rogger	/bragɚ/ → /ragɚ/		0	1
	12. glem → lem	/glɛm/ → /lɛm/		0	1
	13. hidot → idot	/haɪdat/ → /aɪdat/		0	1
	14. wookup → ookup	/wukʌp/ → /ukʌp/		0	1

(continued)

Item	Phonetic spelling	Spoken response	Score	
15. cramset → ramset	/kræmsɛt/ → /ræmsɛt/		0	1
16. frab → rab	/fræb/ →/ræb/		0	1
17. slooslom → looslom	/sluslɑm/ → /luslɑm/		0	1
18. repuze → epuze	/ripjuz/ → /ipjuz/		0	1
19. strid → trid	/strɪd/ →/trɪd/		0	1
20. strat → trat	/stræt/ →/træt/		0	1
21. striggler → triggler	/strɪglɚ/ → /trɪglɚ/		0	1
22. chapet → apet	/ʧæpət/ → /æpət/		0	1

Total score: ______ / 22

Qualitative observations:

SUBTEST 3: Story Retelling (SR)

Note: Subtest 3 can be used as a stand-alone measure or in conjunction with Subtest 9. If administered together with Subtest 9, Subtest 3 must be administered approximately 20–30 minutes before Subtest 9, with language-related activities intervening.

Average time to administer: 4 minutes

Materials: Audio recording device (recommended), Age 6–11 Story 3A, Age 12–18 Story 3B

Start rule: ➡ Arrows with age ranges in years indicate which story to administer

Repetition: No (unless ambient noise interferes)

Basal rule: None

Ceiling rule: None

Directions Select the age-appropriate story and follow the directions for that story.

Probes If the student does not initiate the story, say, ***"Just tell me anything you remember."***

Recording & Scoring

- **Score 1** for each Content Unit the student recalls.
- Count acceptable semantic substitutions as correct (e.g., *obese, chunky* for *fat*). Write in any variations.
- **Score 0** for variations that change the meaning (e.g., *gave* for *traded*).
- Count pronouns correct, but to get credit for *first mention* the student *must* say the characters' proper names (e.g., *Tommy, Michael, Angie*).
- Count Content Units told out of sequence as correct.
- Add the circled **1**s to compute the total score.

Comprehension questions

- After the student's retelling, ask the comprehension questions and record the student's responses verbatim.
- These questions are not part of the quantitative score but can indicate the student's ability to comprehend narratives, draw inferences, and understand idioms.

6–11 STORY 3A: "TOMMY THE TRICKSTER"

Directions

- Begin audio recording (recommended). Say, ***"I'm going to read you a story called 'Tommy the Trickster.' Listen carefully. Your job is to tell the story back to me just like I tell it to you. I can only read it once. Any questions?"*** (Answer.) ***"Let's begin."***
- Read the age-appropriate story, starting with its title, with a natural rate and tone.

"Tommy's mother thought he was getting fat from eating too much junk food. So, she stocked the refrigerator with fruit and carrot sticks. She even put these things in his lunchbox. But Tommy was a fast talker. At school he convinced his friends that cookies were bad for them. Then he traded his fruit and carrots for their cookies. His mother didn't know why Tommy kept gaining weight when all she had given him were healthy foods."

- Say, ***"Now tell me the same story. Start now."***

Content Units	Score	
1. Tommy's (must use proper name to count on first instance)	0	1
2. mother	0	1
3. thought he (Tommy, worried)	0	1
4. was getting fat (bigger, gaining weight)	0	1
5. from eating	0	1
6. too much	0	1
7. junk food (cookies)	0	1
8. so she	0	1
9. stocked (put)	0	1
10. the refrigerator (fridge, icebox)	0	1
11. fruit (healthy foods [only scores once] [not grapes, etc.*])	0	1
12. carrots (carrot sticks, healthy foods, vegetables)	0	1
13. she even put	0	1
14. these things	0	1
15. in his lunchbox (lunch bag, lunch)	0	1
16. but Tommy (he)	0	1
17. was a "fast talker" (figurative meaning)	0	1

Content Units	Score	
18. at school	0	1
19. he convinced (talked them into, told)	0	1
20. his friends	0	1
21. that cookies	0	1
22. were bad	0	1
23. for them	0	1
24. then he traded	0	1
25. his fruit (healthy foods [only scores once])	0	1
26. carrots (carrot sticks, healthy foods)	0	1
27. for cookies	0	1
28. his mother	0	1
29. didn't know why	0	1
30. Tommy (he)	0	1
31. kept gaining weight (getting bigger/fatter)	0	1
32. when all she had given him	0	1
33. were healthy foods	0	1

Total score: _____ **/ 33**

*The scoring guideline is that a child can get credit for a superordinate category label (*vegetables* for *carrots*) but not a more specific one (e.g., *grapes* for *fruit* does not earn credit).

(continued)

Note: Do not forget to administer the comprehension questions on the next page.

Comprehension Questions

Question	Score	
1. Why did Tommy's mother worry about him?		
She thought he was getting fat/gaining weight.	0	1
2. How did Tommy trick his mother?		
By trading his healthy foods for his friends' cookies.	0	1
3. Why did Tommy's mother feel confused?		
Because she was giving him healthy foods but he was still gaining weight.	0	1
4. In the story you heard that Tommy was a fast talker. What do you think that meant?		
He was good at talking people into things/convincing/persuasive (*not* he could talk very fast).	0	1

Note: Credit variations that maintain the intended meaning

Comprehension questions score: ______ / 4

Qualitative observations:

(continued)

12+ **STORY 3B: "THE RUBBER RAFT"**

Directions

- Begin audio recording (recommended). Say, ***"I'm going to read you a story called 'The Rubber Raft.' Listen carefully. Your job is to tell the story back to me just like I tell it to you. I can only read it once. Any questions?"*** (Answer.) ***"Let's begin."***
- Read the age-appropriate story, starting with its title, with a natural rate and tone.

"Last summer, Michael and Angie decided to go to the lake at the park. When they got there, they asked the activity leader if they could use one of the rubber rafts. He said they could if they would pump it up. By the time they finished inflating the raft, Michael and Angie were tired and thirsty, so they left the raft by the lake while they went to the snack bar for a drink. As they were walking back, they spotted a huge gray cat with its claws out getting ready to pounce on the raft. They started running toward the raft, yelling at the cat. But, by the time they got there, it was too late. They were looking at a rubber pancake."

- Say, ***"Now tell me the same story. Start now."***

Content Units	Score	
1. (last) summer	0	1
2. Michael (must use proper name)	0	1
3. Angie (must use proper name)	0	1
4. went	0	1
5. to the lake (beach)	0	1
6. at the park	0	1
7. when they got there	0	1
8. they asked	0	1
9. activity	0	1
10. leader (accept synonyms [only scores once])	0	1
11. if they could use	0	1
12. one	0	1
13. of the rubber rafts	0	1
14. he said	0	1
15. they could (yes)	0	1
16. if they would	0	1
17. pump it up (blow it up, inflate it)	0	1
18. by the time	0	1
19. they finished	0	1
20. inflating (pumping up, blowing it up)	0	1
21. the raft (rubber boat, rubber thing)	0	1
22. Michael (the kids/they [only scores once])	0	1
23. Angie (the kids)	0	1
24. were tired	0	1
25. and thirsty	0	1
26. so they left	0	1

Content Units	Score	
27. the raft	0	1
28. by the lake	0	1
29. while they went	0	1
30. to the snack bar	0	1
31. for a drink	0	1
32. as (while/when)	0	1
33. they were walking back	0	1
34. they spotted (saw)	0	1
35. a huge (large)	0	1
36. gray	0	1
37. cat	0	1
38. with claws out	0	1
39. getting ready	0	1
40. to pounce	0	1
41. on the raft	0	1
42. they started running	0	1
43. toward the raft	0	1
44. yelling at	0	1
45. the cat	0	1
46. (but) by the time (when)	0	1
47. they got there	0	1
48. it was too late	0	1
49. they were looking at	0	1
50. a rubber	0	1
51. pancake	0	1

Total score: ______ / 51

(continued)

Note: Do not forget to administer the comprehension questions on the next page.

Comprehension Questions

Question	Score	
1. What did Michael and Angie ask the activity leader?		
If they could borrow a raft	0	1
2. What did the activity leader tell them they had to do?		
Pump it up/inflate the raft	0	1
3. Why were they tired and thirsty?		
Because they worked hard to blow up the raft	0	1
4. In the story you heard that Michael and Angie saw a rubber pancake. What do you think that meant?		
The raft was flat/looked like a pancake/the cat popped the raft	0	1

Comprehension questions score: ______ /4

Qualitative observations:

SUBTEST 4: **Nonword Repetition (NWRep)**

Note: Subtest 4 can be used as a stand-alone measure or in conjunction with Subtest 5. If administered together with Subtest 5, Subtest 4 must be administered immediately before Subtest 5 and in the same session.

Average time to administer: 4 minutes

Materials: Audio player, *Digital Audio Files* (Tracks 2–28), audio recording device (recommended)

Start rule: ➡ Start at the beginning for all students

Repetition: No (unless ambient noise interferes)

Basal rule: None

Ceiling rule: Scores 0 on 6 out of 8 consecutive items

Directions

- Say, ***"I am going to play a voice recording for you. The person on the recording will say a pretend word that is not a real word. You will only hear the word once. Listen carefully so you can say the word just like the person you hear."*** Say, ***"Any questions?"*** (Answer.) ***"Let's begin."***
- Start playing the audio files and begin recording the student's responses. Pause the recording between tracks if you need more time to record any changes the student makes from the intended response.

Probes

None

Recording & Scoring

- Record the student's response by marking any variations (additions, deletions, or substitutions) not allowed on the scoring form.
- **Score 1** if the student's repetition meets scoring guidelines. **Score 0** if the student's production does not match a variant on the scoring form. (Do not penalize misarticulation of a phoneme if it is consistent with a student's spontaneous speech.)
- Count the number of **1**s and enter as the total score.
- Do not penalize for consistent articulation patterns or regional vowel pronunciations.

Practice Items

Item	Actual/target spoken response
bup	______ /b ʌ p/
stam	______ /s t æ m/

Subtest Items

Item	Actual/target spoken response	Imitation score	
6–18 ➡ 1. gid	______ /g ɪ d/	0	1
2. stenders	______ /s t ɛ n d ɚ z/ /s t ɪ n d ɚ z/	0	1
3. vilding	______ /v ɪ l d ɪ ŋ/	0	1
4. tep	______ /t ɛ p/	0	1
5. dabe	______ /d e͡ɪ b/	0	1
6. tarbing	______ /t ɑr b ɪ ŋ/	0	1
7. skeap	______ /s k i p/	0	1
8. disvagle	______ /d ɪ s v e͡ɪ g l̩/	0	1
9. glapped	______ /g l æ p t/	0	1
10. untigament	______ /ʌ n t ɪ g ə m ɪ n t/ /ʌ n t ɪ g ə m ə n t/	0	1
11. scroil	______ /s k r ɔɪ l/	0	1
12. droof	______ /d r u f/ /d r ʊ f/	0	1
13. interpidable	______ /ɪ n t ɚ p ɪ d ə b l̩/	0	1
14. intosition	______ /ɪ n t o z ɪ ʃ ə n/	0	1
15. smitchly	______ /s m ɪ t͡ʃ l i/	0	1
16. strenopious	______ /s t r ɛ n o p i ə s/ /s t r ɪ n o p i ə s/	0	1

(continued)

Item	Actual/target spoken response	Imitation score	
17. vopiphonia	______ /v o p ɪ f o n i ə/	0	1
18. mistudge	______ /m ɪ s t ʌ ʤ/	0	1
19. dopinician	______ /d o p ə n ɪ ʃ ə n/	0	1
20. nalted	______ /n ɔ l t ə d/ /n ɑ l t ə d/	0	1

Item	Actual/target spoken response	Imitation score	
21. nyvology	______ /n a͞ɪ v ɑ l ə ʤ i/	0	1
22. vattle	______ /v æ t l̩/ [vocalic l] /v æ ɾ l̩/ [flap]	0	1
23. proderopia	______ /p r o d ɚ o p i ə/	0	1
24. transvathial	______ /t r æ n z v e͞ɪ θ i ə l/	0	1

Total score: ______ / 24

Qualitative observations:

SUBTEST 5: Nonword Spelling (NWSpell)

Note: Subtest 4 must be administered immediately prior to Subtest 5 and in the same session.

Average time to administer: 6 minutes

Materials: *Student Response Form* (p. 2), pencil with eraser, audio player, *Digital Audio Files* (Tracks 29–55)

Start rule: ➡ Start at the beginning for all students. (Do not administer Subtest 5 to children age 6;0–6;5.)

Repetition: No (unless ambient noise interferes)

Basal rule: None

Ceiling rule: Scores 0 on 6 out of 8 consecutive items

Directions

- Say, ***"I am going to play another voice recording of pretend words. These are the same words you said before. This time your job is to spell the words on this page*** [point to *Student Response Form*]. ***Remember, these are not real words, but they are like real words. So, use what you know about words to spell these pretend words the best you can. There are two for practice."***
- Pause after each practice item and coach as necessary.
- Say, ***"Any questions?"*** (Answer.) ***"Let's begin."*** Start playing the test items in the audio files and begin scoring the student's responses on the *Examiner Record Form.* Pause the recording between tracks if you need more time to record any changes the student makes from the intended response.

Probes

None

Recording & Scoring

- Transcribe the student's response from the *Student Response Form* and mark any variations (additions, deletions, or substitutions) not allowed on the scoring form.
- **Score 1** if the student's spelling meets scoring guidelines. **Score 0** if the student's spelling does not match a variant on the scoring form. Letter reversals count as errors.
- Count the number of **1**s and enter as the total score.

Practice Items

Item	Child's written response
bup	b u p
stam	s t a m mb

Subtest Items

Item	Child's written response	Spelling score	
➡ 6;6–18 1. gid	g i d	0	1
2. stenders	s t en d er s in z	0	1
3. vilding	v i l d ing ui	0	1
4. tep	t e p	0	1
5. dabe	d a_e b (dabe)* ai b *(*not* daeb)	0	1
6. tarbing	t a r b ing	0	1
7. skeap	s k ea p ee e_e (skepe)	0	1
8. disvagle	dis v a g le f ei el ai al	0	1
9. glapped	g l a pped pt	0	1
10. untigament	un t i g a ment i mant mint	0	1
11. scroil	s c r oi l k oy al le	0	1
12. droof	d r oo f u_e (drufe) ou	0	1

(continued)

Item	Child's written response	Spelling score	
13. interpidable	inter p i d able intra t ible intre tt	0	1
14. intosition	in t o s i tion z sion cian	0	1
15. smitchly	s m i tch ly ch lie ley	0	1
16. strenopious	s t r en o p ious in ias an ius eous	0	1
17. vopiphonia	v o p i phonia o fonia a	0	1
18. mistudge	mis t u dge	0	1
19. dopinician	d o p i n i cian a tion o sion	0	1
20. nalted	n a l t ed kn au gn aw	0	1
21. nyvology	n y v ology kn i	0	1
22. vattle	v a tt le dd el	0	1
23. proderopia	pro d er o p ia t or	0	1
24. transvathial	trans v a th ial ai iel	0	1

Total score: _____ / 24

Qualitative observations:

SUBTEST 6: Listening Comprehension (LC)

Note: Subtest 6 can be used as a stand-alone measure or in conjunction with Subtest 7. If administered together with Subtest 7, Subtest 6 must be administered immediately before Subtest 7 and in the same session.

Average time to administer: 7 minutes

Materials: None

Start rule: ➡ Start points for age ranges are indicated by arrows

Repetition: No (except for practice story or if ambient noise interferes)

Basal rule: All 3 items correct for 2 consecutive stories

Ceiling rule: All 3 items incorrect for 2 consecutive stories

Directions

- Say, ***"I'm going to read some very short stories. Pay careful attention because I'm going to ask you some questions after each story. Tell me 'yes' if you are sure the answer is 'yes.' Tell me 'no' if you are sure the answer is 'no.' If the story doesn't clearly tell you the answer, tell me 'maybe.' Some stories will not have all three kinds of answers—yes, no, and maybe. Here's one for practice."***
- Read Practice Item. Coach "maybe" for Practice Item c, if needed, by asking ***"Are you sure Teresa does/does not have a dog? The story didn't really tell us the answer."***
- Say, ***"Any questions?"*** (Answer.) ***"Let's begin."***

Probes Do not define the words. If the student indicates non-understanding, say, ***"It's okay to take a guess."***

Recording & Scoring

- Circle Y if the child answers "yes." Circle N if the child answers "no." Circle M if the child answers "maybe."
- **Score 1** if the child's response matches the answer shown in parentheses. **Score 0** if it does not.
- Count the number of **1**s and enter as the total score.

Practice Item

Teresa has a gray and white kitten that likes to play with string. The kitten's name is Fluffy.			
a. Is Teresa's kitten black?	Y	**(N)**	M
b. Does Teresa's kitten like to play with string?	**(Y)**	N	M
c. Does Teresa have a dog?	Y	N	**(M)**

Subtest Items

6–11 ➡

1. The guy who makes the pizza crust can toss it in the air and catch it, but last night he had a little accident. He ended up with pizza dough hanging over his head.					
a. Is the pizza maker always successful?	Y	**(N)**	M	0	1
b. Was he able to make some good crust last night?	Y	N	**(M)**	0	1
c. Did he ruin some crust last night?	**(Y)**	N	M	0	1

12+ ➡

2. Cassandra sat on the couch and got ready to watch the movie she liked best while her babysitter went into the kitchen to make popcorn. She had asked her babysitter to make cheese popcorn, but the babysitter brought back caramel popcorn instead. Cassandra exclaimed, "I didn't know you could make caramel popcorn. Caramel is my favorite!"					
a. Did Cassandra help make popcorn?	Y	**(N)**	M	0	1
b. Was Cassandra getting ready to watch her favorite movie?	**(Y)**	N	M	0	1
c. Had Cassandra asked her babysitter to make caramel popcorn?	Y	**(N)**	M	0	1

3. The class did not understand the teacher's directions when she first told them how to complete the science project. When she showed them what to do step by step, however, the instructions made more sense.					
a. Did all of the students understand the directions after the teacher's demonstration?	Y	N	**(M)**	0	1
b. Did the students know what to do at first?	Y	**(N)**	M	0	1
c. Did the class complete the assignment?	Y	N	**(M)**	0	1

(continued)

4. Immanuel was the first one of a small group of boys in his class who could dunk a basketball.					
a. Could some of the other boys dunk a basketball?	**(Y)**	N	M	0	1
b. Could all of the boys in Immanuel's class dunk a basketball?	Y	**(N)**	M	0	1
c. Was Immanuel the best basketball player in the class?	Y	N	**(M)**	0	1

5. We thought it was strange that the art teacher told us to clean the brushes before we started painting. But when we realized that they really needed it, we followed his instructions.					
a. Were the brushes dirty at first?	**(Y)**	N	M	0	1
b. Did we clean the brushes after we finished?	Y	N	**(M)**	0	1
c. Was the art teacher a woman?	Y	**(N)**	M	0	1

6. The land beyond the mountains was divided into two new territories. Each was to have its own governor, who would be selected by the President following consultation with his advisors.					
a. Was a different governor going to be appointed for each new territory?	**(Y)**	N	M	0	1
b. Were the mountains part of the new territories?	Y	**(N)**	M	0	1
c. Was the President in charge of choosing the new governors?	**(Y)**	N	M	0	1

7. I asked Dan's sister why she was planning to take an umbrella to the beach. She said that if it rained, the umbrella would keep her dry, but if the sun was shining, it would protect her from the harmful rays.					
a. Did Dan's sister forget her umbrella?	Y	N	**(M)**	0	1
b. Does Dan's sister think about things ahead of time?	**(Y)**	N	M	0	1
c. Did Dan's sister go alone to the beach?	Y	N	**(M)**	0	1

8. Mary and Todd decided they would go to the beach on Saturday even if it was a cloudy day. When they woke up on Saturday, it was sunny.					
a. Did Mary and Todd plan to go to the beach on Saturday if it was cloudy?	**(Y)**	N	M	0	1
b. Did it rain later on Saturday?	Y	N	**(M)**	0	1
c. Was it cloudy when Mary and Todd woke up on Saturday?	Y	**(N)**	M	0	1

9. The scientists observed the insects closely over a 24-hour period, hoping to study their swarming behavior. At that point, the scientists concluded that the insects had been prevented from swarming because of the unusual atmospheric conditions.					
a. Did the insects swarm during the observation period?	Y	**(N)**	M	0	1
b. Can atmospheric conditions influence the swarming of insects?	**(Y)**	N	M	0	1
c. Did the scientists accomplish their original goal?	Y	**(N)**	M	0	1

Total score: ______ / 27

Qualitative observations:

SUBTEST 7: Reading Comprehension (RC)

Note: Subtest 6 must be administered immediately prior to Subtest 7 and in the same session.

Average time to administer: 8 minutes

Materials: *Student Response Form* (p. 3), pencil with eraser, cardstock (optional)

Start rule: ➡ Start points for age ranges are indicated by arrows; however, start with Story 1 if you suspect a student to have a reading decoding problem. (Do not administer to children age 6;0-6;5.)

Repetition: Not applicable

Basal rule: All 3 items correct for 2 consecutive stories

Ceiling rule: All 3 items incorrect for 2 consecutive stories

Screening rule: If a student misreads 7 or more words in Story 1 and does not self-correct, discontinue testing.

Directions

- No practice items. (Subtest 6 provides the practice for Subtest 7.)
- Say, ***"Now, it's your turn to read some short stories and answer the questions in your Student Response Form. Circle 'yes' if you are sure the answer is 'yes.' Circle 'no' if you are sure the answer is 'no.' If the story doesn't clearly tell you the answer, circle 'maybe.' You may choose to hold the card under each line as you read it. Please read the first story aloud."***
- Have the student read Story 1 aloud. Mark any words the student misreads (or does not self-correct). If the student misreads 7 or more words, discontinue Subtest 7, score 0 for this subtest, and write in "emergent reader."
- If you have any doubt about the student's reading decoding ability, regardless of age, use the screening rule.
- Say, ***"Any questions?"*** (Answer.) ***"Let's begin."*** The student may read silently or aloud after Subtest Item 1.

Probes Do not define the words or help with decoding. If the student indicates non-understanding, say, ***"It's okay to take a guess."***

Recording & Scoring

- The student circles his or her own answers in the *Student Response Form.* Transcribe the student's responses in the *Examiner Record Form.*
- **Score 1** if the student's response matches the answer shown in boldface.
- **Score 0** if it does not.
- Score any unanswered items 0.
- Count the number of **1**s and enter as the total score. Score the Subtest 0 if the student misreads 7 or more words when attempting to read the first story aloud.

Subtest Items

➡ 6;6–11

1. "What I Did on My Summer Vacation" is the topic the teacher makes her class write about the first day of school every year. When school started a month ago, the teacher gave her usual first writing assignment.					
a. Was "The Middle East" the first writing assignment?	Y	**(N)**	M	0	1
b. Did all of the students take a trip on their summer vacation?	Y	N	**(M)**	0	1
c. Did the teacher ask her class to write about their summer vacations?	**(Y)**	N	M	0	1

2. Last summer, Renaldo and Jake had fun in summer school learning new things. Photography was Renaldo's favorite class; in fact, the picture that Renaldo took of his friend Jake won the summer school prize.					
a. Did Jake win the summer school prize?	Y	**(N)**	M	0	1
b. Did Jake take a picture?	Y	N	**(M)**	0	1
c. Did both boys have a good time in summer school?	**(Y)**	N	M	0	1

➡ 12–14

3. Anna was excited when she thought about playing with her new hamster every day. However, she was surprised when she discovered that her hamster sleeps all day and runs on his wheel all night.					
a. Does Anna's hamster sleep all night?	Y	**(N)**	M	0	1
b. Did Anna expect her hamster to sleep all day before she brought him home?	Y	**(N)**	M	0	1
c. Does Anna's hamster keep her awake all night?	Y	N	**(M)**	0	1

➡ 15+

4. All his friends thought that Carlos looked better before he had his hair cut by Juan.					
a. Is Juan a barber?	Y	N	**(M)**	0	1
b. Did Carlos's friends think Juan's haircut improved Carlos's looks?	Y	**(N)**	M	0	1
c. Did Carlos like his new haircut?	Y	N	**(M)**	0	1

5. One morning Susan got up too late to catch the school bus. She thought that she would be late for school, but her mother got her there on time.					
a. Did Susan miss the bus?	**(Y)**	N	M	0	1
b. Was it raining that morning?	Y	N	**(M)**	0	1
c. Did Susan expect to miss the start of the school day?	**(Y)**	N	M	0	1

(continued)

6. The sport Eddie likes to play best is soccer. He can kick a soccer ball the second farthest in his class and run faster than anybody in his class.					
a. Can Eddie kick a soccer ball farther than anyone else in his class?	Y	**(N)**	M	0	1
b. Does Eddie like to play baseball?	Y	N	**(M)**	0	1
c. Does Eddie run the fastest in his class?	**(Y)**	N	M	0	1

7. The scientists observed the insects closely over a 24-hour period, hoping to study their swarming behavior. At that point, the scientists concluded that the insects had been prevented from swarming because of the unusual atmospheric conditions.					
a. Did the insects swarm during the observation period?	Y	**(N)**	M	0	1
b. Can atmospheric conditions influence the swarming of insects?	**(Y)**	N	M	0	1
c. Did the scientists draw a conclusion even though the study did not go exactly as planned?	**(Y)**	N	M	0	1

Total score: _____ / 21

Qualitative observations:

Place a checkmark beside strategies observed:

___ Moving the card from line to line

___ Scanning left to right

___ Looking back to the story

Other:

SUBTEST 8: Following Directions (FD)

Average time to administer: 8 minutes
Materials: *Student Response Form* (pp. 4–6), pencil with eraser, cardstock
Start rule: ➡ Start points for age ranges are indicated by arrows
Repetition: No (unless ambient noise interferes)
Basal rule: 6 consecutive scores of 1
Ceiling rule: Scores 0 on 6 out of 8 consecutive items

Directions

- Sit in a position where you can easily observe the child's responses in the *Student Response Form.*
- Cover up the first practice item in the *Student Response Form* with the cardstock. Say, ***"I'm going to give you some directions to follow with your pencil in your Student Response Form. Listen carefully because I can only say them once. When I say 'Go,' move the card and use your pencil to follow the directions exactly as I told you."***
- ***"We will try two for practice."*** Say, ***"Practice number 1: Cross out the circle. Go."*** Proceed to practice number 2.
- Say, ***"Any questions?"*** (Answer.) ***"Let's begin."***
- Continue to cover the stimulus items while the child listens to the directions for each item.

Probes

None

Recording & Scoring

- Watch the student's response carefully so you can record it accurately in the *Examiner Record Form.* **Use arrows to show the direction** of the student's action, and **number the order of actions** to show the sequence.
- **Score 1** if the student follows all directions (represented in purple). If sequence (order of responses) is specified in the directions, the student must perform the actions in the order requested.
- If any part of the response to these directions is in error, **score 0.**
- Count the number of **1**s and enter as the total score.

Practice Items

Instructions	Student's response (from *Student Response Form*)
Number 1: Cross out the circle. Go. [Either an X or single line may be used to "cross out."]	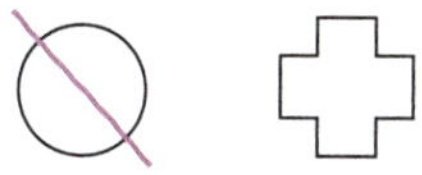
Number 2: Draw an arrow from the heart to the box. Go.	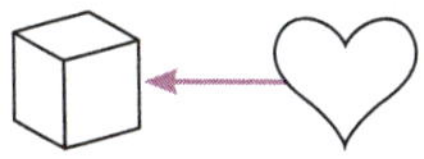

Subtest Items

Start	Instructions	Student's response (from *Student Response Form*)	Score	
6–9	Number 1: Draw a circle around the heart. Go.		0	1
	Number 2: Cross out the lion and circle the star. Go. [Either an X or single line may be used to "cross out."]	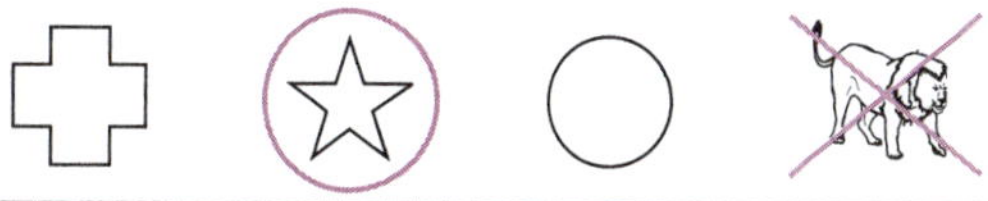	0	1
	Number 3: Draw a line from the top of the tree to the bottom of the light bulb. Go.	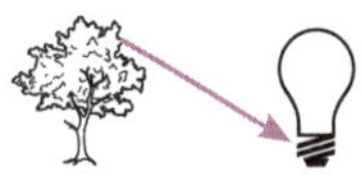	0	1
	Number 4: Draw hair on the sad face and put a nose on the happy face. Go.		0	1
10–14	Number 5: When you have finished circling all the stars, cross out the square. Go. [Sequence] [Say, ***"Turn the page."***]		0	1
	Number 6: Draw a line above the tree and circle the lock. Go. [Line may be horizontal or vertical.]		0	1

(continued)

Instructions	Student's response (from *Student Response Form*)	Score	
Number 7: If the lock is in the middle, underline the star. If not, circle the tree. Go.		0	1
Number 8: If there is an arrow pointing down, draw a circle under the moon. If not, circle the star. Go.		0	1
Number 9: If there is a number 3, underline the B. If not, circle the X. Go.	3 X W 7 B	0	1
15+ Number 10: Before you cross out the cloud, draw an arrow from the light bulb over the cloud to the box. Go. [Sequence] [Line through the cloud does not count]	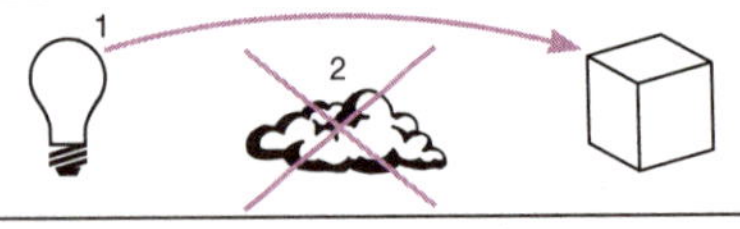	0	1
Number 11: Write a letter F above the frog, an L above the lion, and then an H above the horse. Go. [Lowercase is acceptable.] [Sequence]		0	1
Number 12: Circle the star then the moon, but before that, draw a line between them. Go. [Line may be horizontal or vertical.] [Sequence]	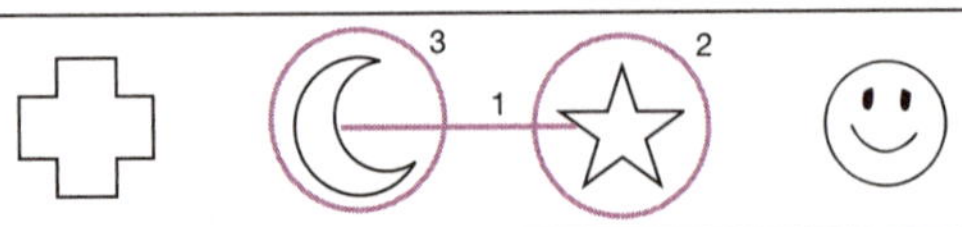	0	1
Number 13: Before you cross out the sun, underline the triangle and then the cross. Go. [Sequence] [Say, ***"Turn the page."***]		0	1
Number 14: Write a number 1 in the first shape on the left, a 2 in the center shape, and a 3 in the last shape on the right. Cross out the other 2 shapes. Go.		0	1
Number 15: Write a letter S in the circle in the middle, cross out the S that is inside the square, and circle the S that is outside the square. Go.		0	1
Number 16: After you give the happy face a nose, put a dot in the center of the triangle and the cross. Then underline the star. Go. [Sequence]	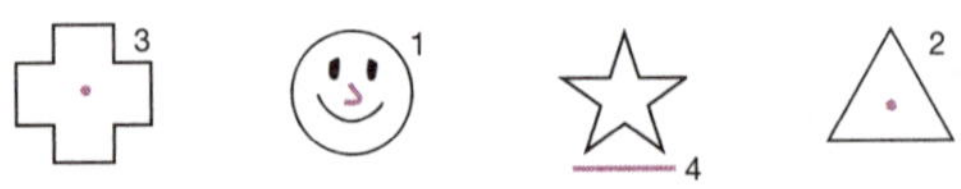	0	1
Number 17: Start by circling the books. Then draw a line from the top of the books under the tree and into the center of the star. Go. [Sequence]	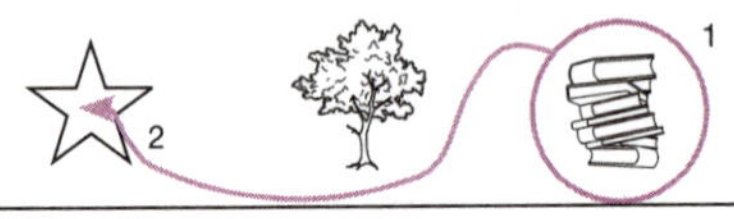	0	1
Number 18: Draw a line from the lightning bolt over the moon and into the sun. Then draw a circle under the arrow. Go. [Sequence] [Line through moon does not count.]	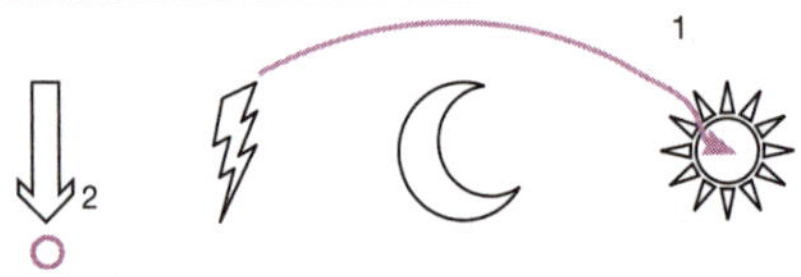	0	1
Number 19: Cross out the largest number and draw a line from the lowercase e to the S over the number between them. Go.	E 88 e 20 S 16	0	1
Number 20: Underline both Fs. Draw a line over the 2, and cross out the A. Go. [Line over the 2 may be horizontal or vertical.]	2 f a C F	0	1

Total score: _____ **/ 20**

Qualitative observations:

SUBTEST 9: Delayed Story Retelling (DSR)

Note: Subtest 9 must be administered approximately 20–30 minutes following Subtest 3, with language-related activities intervening.

Average time to administer: 2 minutes

Materials: Audio recording device (recommended)

Start rule: ➡ Arrows with age ranges in years indicate which story to administer

Repetition: Not applicable

Basal rule: None

Ceiling rule: None

Directions Select the age-appropriate story and follow the directions for that story for the student to tell the story again.

Probes If the student does not initiate the story, say, ***"Just tell me anything you remember."***

Recording & Scoring

- **Score 1** for each Content Unit the student recalls.
- Count acceptable semantic substitutions as correct.
- Do not count variations that change the meaning as correct.
- Count pronouns correct, but to get credit for *first mention* the student *must* say the characters' proper names (e.g., *Tommy, Michael, Angie*).
- Count Content Units told out of sequence as correct.
- Add the circled **1**s to compute the total score.

6–11 ➡ STORY A: "TOMMY THE TRICKSTER"

Directions

- Begin audio recording (recommended).
- Turn to the age-appropriate story and say, ***"Remember the story 'Tommy the Trickster'? Tell me that story again. Try to remember as much as you can. Any questions?"*** (Answer.) ***"Let's begin."***

Content Units	Score	
1. Tommy's (must use proper name to count on first instance)	0	1
2. mother	0	1
3. thought he (Tommy, worried)	0	1
4. was getting fat (bigger, gaining weight)	0	1
5. from eating	0	1
6. too much	0	1
7. junk food (cookies)	0	1
8. so she	0	1
9. stocked (put)	0	1
10. the refrigerator (fridge, icebox)	0	1
11. fruit (healthy foods [only scores once] [not grapes, etc.*])	0	1
12. carrots (carrot sticks, healthy foods, vegetables)	0	1
13. she even put	0	1
14. these things	0	1
15. in his lunchbox (lunch bag, lunch)	0	1
16. but Tommy (he)	0	1
17. was a "fast talker" (figurative meaning)	0	1

Content Units	Score	
18. at school	0	1
19. he convinced (talked them into, told)	0	1
20. his friends	0	1
21. that cookies	0	1
22. were bad	0	1
23. for them	0	1
24. then he traded	0	1
25. his fruit (healthy foods [only scores once])	0	1
26. carrots (carrot sticks, healthy foods)	0	1
27. for cookies	0	1
28. his mother	0	1
29. didn't know why	0	1
30. Tommy (he)	0	1
31. kept gaining weight (getting bigger/fatter)	0	1
32. when all she had given him	0	1
33. were healthy foods	0	1

*The scoring guideline is that a child can get credit for a superordinate category label (*vegetables* for *carrots*) but not a more specific one (e.g., *grapes* for *fruit* does not earn credit).

Total score: _____ **/ 33**

Qualitative observations:

(continued)

12+

STORY B: "THE RUBBER RAFT"

Directions

- Begin audio recording (recommended).
- Turn to the age-appropriate story and say, ***"Remember the story 'The Rubber Raft'? Tell me that story again. Try to remember as much as you can. Any questions?"*** (Answer.) ***"Let's begin."***

Content Units	Score	
1. (last) summer	0	1
2. Michael (must use proper name)	0	1
3. Angie (must use proper name)	0	1
4. went	0	1
5. to the lake (beach)	0	1
6. at the park	0	1
7. when they got there	0	1
8. they asked	0	1
9. activity	0	1
10. leader (accept synonyms [only score once])	0	1
11. if they could use	0	1
12. one	0	1
13. of the rubber rafts	0	1
14. he said	0	1
15. they could (yes)	0	1
16. if they would	0	1
17. pump it up (blow it up, inflate it)	0	1
18. by the time	0	1
19. they finished	0	1
20. inflating (pumping up, blowing it up)	0	1
21. the raft (rubber boat, rubber thing)	0	1
22. Michael (the kids/they [only scores once])	0	1
23. Angie (the kids)	0	1
24. were tired	0	1
25. and thirsty	0	1
26. so they left	0	1

Content Units	Score	
27. the raft	0	1
28. by the lake	0	1
29. while they went	0	1
30. to the snack bar	0	1
31. for a drink	0	1
32. as (while/when)	0	1
33. they were walking back	0	1
34. they spotted (saw)	0	1
35. a huge (large)	0	1
36. gray	0	1
37. cat	0	1
38. with claws out	0	1
39. getting ready	0	1
40. to pounce	0	1
41. on the raft	0	1
42. they started running	0	1
43. toward the raft	0	1
44. yelling at	0	1
45. the cat	0	1
46. (but) by the time (when)	0	1
47. they got there	0	1
48. it was too late	0	1
49. they were looking at	0	1
50. a rubber	0	1
51. pancake	0	1

Total score: ______ / 51

Qualitative observations:

SUBTEST 10: **Nonword Reading (NWRead)**

Average time to administer: 4 minutes

Materials: *Stimulus Book* (pp. 57–67), audio recording device (recommended)

Start rule: ➡ Start points for age ranges are indicated by arrows. (Do not administer to children age 6;0–6;5.)

Repetition: Not applicable

Basal rule: 6 consecutive scores of 1

Ceiling rule: Scores 0 on 6 out of 8 consecutive items

Directions

- Begin audio recording (recommended).
- Say, ***"Here are some words for you to read aloud."*** [Indicate practice words on page 57 of the *Stimulus Book*.] ***"These are pretend words that are not real words, but they are like real words. Your job is to read these words aloud. My job is to write what you say, so wait until I say 'Next' before you read the next word. Here are two for practice."***
- Even if you have to return to a previous page to establish basal, have the student start reading at the top of the page. If the student reaches ceiling in the middle of the page, have the student read all words on that page before stopping.
- Say, ***"Any questions?"*** (Answer.) ***"Let's begin."***

Probes If a response has not been provided after 5 seconds, say, ***"Give it a try."*** If no attempt at a response is made, record 0 for that item and move on to the next. Encourage the student to attempt the words for this subtest even if he or she is an emergent reader.

Recording & Scoring

- **Score 1** if the student correctly produces the word or one of the acceptable alternatives shown on the scoring sheet.
- **Score 0** if the student makes any changes in the word other than those allowed and record the student's exact response in the space provided using traditional orthography or phonetic spelling.
- Record changes in syllable stress for qualitative analysis but do not consider stress variation when judging correctness.
- The goal in this test is to credit accurate decoding (which may not be fluent decoding), so score the student's final attempt.
- Add the circled **1**s to compute the student's total score.

Practice Items

Stimulus word	Expected production (and acceptable alternatives)
gup	________ /gʌp/
rask	________ /ræsk/

Subtest Items

Start	Stimulus word	Expected production (and acceptable alternatives)	Score	
6;6–7	1. pog	________ /pɔg/ /pɑg/	0	1
	2. keb	________ /kɛb/	0	1
	3. troom [Turn the page.]	________ /trum/	0	1
8–10	4. dape	________ /de͡ɪp/	0	1
	5. glenders	________ /glɛn' dɚz/ /glɪn' dɚz/	0	1
	6. sproil [Turn the page.]	________ /sprɔ͡ɪl/	0	1

Start	Stimulus word	Expected production (and acceptable alternatives)	Score	
11–13	7. mistation	________ /mɪs te' ʃən/	0	1
	8. steeg	________ /stig/	0	1
	9. shiggle	________ /ʃɪ' gl̩/	0	1
	10. brapped [Turn the page.]	________ /bræpt/	0	1
14+	11. shreebing	________ /ʃri' bɪŋ/	0	1
	12. tilding	________ /tɪl' dɪŋ/	0	1

(continued)

Stimulus word	Expected production (and acceptable alternatives)	Score	
13. unverly	______ /ʌn' vɚ li/ /ʌn vɚ' li/	0	1
14. ralted	______ /rɔl' təd/	0	1
15. distudge	______ /dɪs tʌʤ'/	0	1
16. gorentobia	______ /go rən to' bi ə/ /go rɛn to' bi ə/	0	1
17. plitchly	______ /plɪʧ' li/	0	1
18. tyvology [Turn the page.]	______ /taɪv ɑ' lə ʤi/	0	1
19. redikament	______ /ri dɪ kə mɪnt/	0	1
20. nopiphonia	______ /no pɪ fo' ni ə/ /nɑ pɪ fo' ni ə/	0	1
21. interdepable	______ /ɪn tɚ dɛp' əbl̩/	0	1
22. smorifious	______ /smor ɪ' fi əs/ /smor ɪ fi' əs/	0	1
23. periothial	______ /per i ɑ' θi əl/ /per i o' θi əl/ /per i o θi' əl/	0	1
24. kizmanician	______ /kɪz mə nɪ' ʃən/	0	1

Total score: ______ **/ 24**

Qualitative observations:

SUBTEST 11: Reading Fluency (RF)

Note: Subtest 11 can be used as a stand-alone measure or in conjunction with Subtest 12. If administered together with Subtest 12, Subtest 11 must be administered immediately before Subtest 12 and in the same session.

Average time to administer: 2 minutes

Materials: *Stimulus Book* (correct story for age), audio recording device (recommended)
Age 6;6–7 Story A (p. 69), Age 8–10 Story B (p. 71), Age 11–13 Story C (p. 73), Age 14–18 Story D (p. 75)

Start rule: ➡ Arrows with age ranges in years indicate which story to administer

Repetition: Not applicable

Basal rule: None

Ceiling rule: If the student becomes upset or anxious, you may decide to discontinue. If so, count any unread words as 0.

Directions

- Begin audio recording (recommended).
- Turn to the age-appropriate story in the *Stimulus Book.* Say, ***"Here are some facts that tell a story. First, read the title out loud."*** Then say, ***"Now read the facts."*** If the student struggles to read any words in the title, say, ***"Just read the words you know. It is okay to skip the words you do not know."***

Probes If the student experiences difficulty, say, ***"Just read the words you know."***

Recording & Scoring

- Mark any word that the student does not read fluently. *Fluent* means without sounding out and with no hesitation, omission, repetition, or change in the intended word. Record any changes or word omissions or additions on the form.
- Score any unread words as 0 if you decide to discontinue due to the student becoming upset or anxious.
- Enter the number of words read fluently for each item. Subtract 1 for any word addition, and calculate the total score.
- If a child repeats a whole phrase, subtract 1 point.

6;6–7

READING FLUENCY SCORING FORM
Story A: "The Class Pet" (p. 69)

Story elements	Score	Story elements	Score
Title: The Class Pet	/3	9. The door was open.	/4
1. The class has a pet.	/5	10. The children looked.	/3
2. It is a hamster.	/4	11. The children found him.	/4
3. The hamster has spots.	/4	12. They put him back.	/4
4. Some are brown.	/3	13. They put him in the cage.	/6
5. Some are white.	/3	14. They closed the door.	/4
6. It got out.	/3	15. He found a corner.	/4
7. It was one day last week.	/6	16. He went to sleep.	/4
8. The cage was open.	/4	Column total	/33
Column total	/35	**Total score**	**/68**

Qualitative observations:

(continued)

Directions

- Begin audio recording (recommended).
- Turn to the age-appropriate story in the *Stimulus Book*. Say, ***"Here are some facts that tell a story. First, read the title out loud."*** If the student can read the title, say, ***"Now read the facts."***

8–10

READING FLUENCY SCORING FORM Story B: "The Principal's Daughter" (p. 71)			
Story elements	**Score**	**Story elements**	**Score**
Title: The Principal's Daughter	/3	11. It was big.	/3
1. We have a principal.	/4	12. She looked scary.	/3
2. The principal has a daughter.	/5	13. She walked into a class.	/5
3. Her name is Sara.	/4	14. The children were young.	/4
4. She wants to be a clown.	/6	15. The children saw her.	/4
5. She came Monday.	/3	16. Some children cried.	/3
6. She came to our school.	/5	17. They were scared.	/3
7. She had on makeup.	/4	18. She took off her wig.	/5
8. She had on a wig.	/5	19. The children were happy.	/4
9. A ball was on her nose.	/6	20. They knew Sara.	/3
10. It was red.	/3	Column total	/37
Column total	/48	**Total score**	**/85**

Qualitative observations:

(continued)

Directions

- Begin audio recording (recommended).
- Turn to the age-appropriate story in the *Stimulus Book*. Say, ***"Here are some facts that tell a story. First, read the title out loud."*** If the student can read the title, say, ***"Now read the facts."***

11–13

READING FLUENCY SCORING FORM Story C: "When the School Closed" (p. 73)			
Story elements	**Score**	**Story elements**	**Score**
Title: When the School Closed	/4	17. There were two.	/3
1. Our school was closed.	/4	18. They were eating cookies.	/4
2. It was last Wednesday.	/4	19. They had eaten many.	/4
3. It was a school day.	/5	20. They looked full.	/3
4. It was closed all day.	/5	21. He called animal control.	/4
5. The janitor came in at 6 a.m.	/7	22. He called right away.	/4
6. He opened the school.	/4	23. The workers came.	/3
7. He smelled something.	/3	24. They took the skunks.	/4
8. It was strong.	/3	25. They let them go.	/4
9. It almost knocked him over.	/5	26. It was in the woods.	/5
10. It was a skunk.	/4	27. The smell stayed.	/3
11. He opened the doors.	/4	28. It was in the building.	/5
12. He left them open.	/4	29. The smell finally left.	/4
13. He searched.	/2	30. It took one week.	/4
14. He looked in the library.	/5	31. The school smelled normal.	/4
15. He looked in the cafeteria.	/5	Column total	/58
16. He found the skunks.	/4	**Total score**	**/130**
Column total	/72		

Qualitative observations:

(continued)

Directions

- Begin audio recording (recommended).
- Turn to the age-appropriate story in the *Stimulus Book*. Say, ***"Here are some facts that tell a story. First, read the title out loud."*** If the student can read the title, say, ***"Now read the facts."***

14+

READING FLUENCY SCORING FORM
Story D: "The Building" (p. 75)

Story elements	Score	Story elements	Score
Title: The Building	/2	18. People did not think about it.	/6
1. There was a building.	/4	19. It was almost hidden.	/4
2. It was old.	/3	20. They did not care.	/4
3. No one knew how old.	/5	21. Then something happened.	/3
4. There were no records.	/4	22. The city wanted the land.	/5
5. People talked about it.	/4	23. They needed a new road.	/5
6. It had a history.	/4	24. The building would be demolished.	/5
7. Some people knew.	/3	25. People suddenly cared.	/3
8. It was used in a war.	/6	26. They wrote articles.	/3
9. It was long ago.	/4	27. They gave speeches.	/3
10. The building was a hospital.	/5	28. They raised money.	/3
11. Soldiers came there.	/3	29. They saved the building.	/4
12. There were hundreds.	/3	30. They saved the grave yard.	/5
13. Many were treated.	/3	31. They saved something else.	/4
14. Many died.	/2	32. It was their history.	/4
15. They were buried.	/3	33. That was more important.	/4
16. The grave yard was still there.	/6	Column total	/65
17. It was behind the building.	/5	**Total score**	**/134**
Column total	/69		

Qualitative observations:

SUBTEST 12: **Written Expression (WE)**

Note: Subtest 11 must be administered immediately prior to Subtest 12 and in the same session.

Average time to administer: 10 minutes

Materials: *Stimulus Book* (p. 77; then correct story for age), *Student Response Form* (p. 8)
Age 6;6–7 Story A (p. 69), Age 8–10 Story B (p. 71), Age 11–13 Story C (p. 73), Age 14–18 Story D (p. 75)

Start rule: Arrows with age ranges in years indicate which story to administer

Repetition: Not applicable

Basal rule: None

Ceiling rule: If the student indicates being finished, record the time spent writing and move to the next subtest

Directions

- Open the *Stimulus Book* to page 77 and the *Student Response Form* to page 7.
- Say, ***"Here's another story. It has facts about a little dog."*** [Read the story "The Little Dog" on page 77 of the *Stimulus Book* out loud to the student.] ***"It's okay, but it sounds choppy. Here is an example of how you could put the facts together to make it sound less choppy and more interesting."*** [Read the sample rewritten story on page 7 of the *Student Response Form*.] ***"Now it's your turn to put the facts for your story together in a way that sounds better."*** [Point to the age-appropriate story in the *Stimulus Book* from Subtest 11. Keep the *Stimulus Book* open for the student during Subtest 12.] ***"You can write your story here.*** [Point to the back page in the *Student Response Form* (p. 8).] ***Be sure you include all the facts. Do you have any questions?"*** (Answer.) ***"Let's begin."***
- If the student showed any problems with reading fluency on Subtest 11, before beginning the writing say, ***"I'm going to read these facts with you again while you follow along."***

Probes If you observe that the student is copying, you can say, ***"Remember that your job is not to copy the story. Your job is to use these facts and put them together in a way that sounds less choppy and more interesting."*** If the student stops writing prematurely, say, ***"You still have some time to work on your story."***

6;6–7

WRITTEN EXPRESSION CONTENT UNITS SCORING FORM **Story A: "The Class Pet" (p. 69)**					
1. The class has a pet.	0	1	9. The door was open.	0	1
2. It is a hamster.	0	1	10. The children looked.	0	1
3. The hamster has spots.	0	1	11. The children found him.	0	1
4. Some are brown.	0	1	12. They put him back.	0	1
5. Some are white.	0	1	13. They put him in the cage.	0	1
6. It got out.	0	1	14. They closed the door.	0	1
7. It was one day last week.	0	1	15. He found a corner.	0	1
8. The cage was open.	0	1	16. He went to sleep.	0	1
				Content Units total	**/16**

Discourse Score	_____ Content Units / 16 possible × 100 = _____% Content Included
Sentence Score	_____ Content Units / _____ T-units* = _____ Sentence Score (record 2 decimal places)
Word Score	_____ Total Words − _____ Error Words = _____ Total Correct Words / _____ Total Words × 100 = _____% Words Correct

****Note:*** For more information about how to calculate T-units, see pages 74–77 in the *Examiner's Manual*.

(continued)

Qualitative observations:

8–10

WRITTEN EXPRESSION CONTENT UNITS SCORING FORM

Story B: "The Principal's Daughter" (p. 71)

1. We have a principal.	0	1	11. It was big.	0	1
2. The principal has a daughter.	0	1	12. She looked scary.	0	1
3. Her name is Sara.	0	1	13. She walked into a class.	0	1
4. She wants to be a clown.	0	1	14. The children were young.	0	1
5. She came Monday.	0	1	15. The children saw her.	0	1
6. She came to our school.	0	1	16. Some children cried.	0	1
7. She had on makeup.	0	1	17. They were scared.	0	1
8. She had on a wig.*	0	1	18. She took off her wig.	0	1
9. A ball was on her nose.	0	1	19. The children were happy.	0	1
10. It was red.	0	1	20. They knew Sara.	0	1
			Content Units total		**/20**

*Note: If child writes "dress" or "attire," score 1 for wig but 0 for makeup or ball on nose.

Discourse Score	____ Content Units / 20 possible × 100 = ____% Content Included
Sentence Score	____ Content Units / ____ T-units* = ____ Sentence Score (record 2 decimal places)
Word Score	____ Total Words – ____ Error Words = ____ Total Correct Words / ____ Total Words × 100 = ____% Words Correct

***Note:** For more information about how to calculate T-units, see pages 74–77 in the *Examiner's Manual*.

Qualitative observations:

11–13

WRITTEN EXPRESSION CONTENT UNITS SCORING FORM

Story C: "When the School Closed" (p. 73)

1. Our school was closed.	0	1	17. There were two.	0	1
2. It was last Wednesday.	0	1	18. They were eating cookies.	0	1
3. It was a school day.	0	1	19. They had eaten many.	0	1
4. It was closed all day.	0	1	20. They looked full.	0	1
5. The janitor came in at 6 a.m.	0	1	21. He called animal control.	0	1
6. He opened the school.	0	1	22. He called right away.	0	1
7. He smelled something.	0	1	23. The workers came.	0	1
8. It was strong.	0	1	24. They took the skunks.	0	1
9. It almost knocked him over. (figurative meaning)	0	1	25. They let them go.	0	1
10. It was a skunk.	0	1	26. It was in the woods.	0	1
11. He opened the doors.	0	1	27. The smell stayed.	0	1
12. He left them open.	0	1	28. It was in the building.	0	1
13. He searched. (looked in)	0	1	29. The smell finally left.	0	1
14. He looked in the library.	0	1	30. It took one week.	0	1
15. He looked in the cafeteria.	0	1	31. The school smelled normal.	0	1
16. He found the skunks.	0	1	**Content Units total**		**/31**

Discourse Score	____ Content Units / 31 possible × 100 = ____% Content Included
Sentence Score	____ Content Units / ____ T-units* = ____ Sentence Score (record 2 decimal places)
Word Score	____ Total Words – ____ Error Words = ____ Total Correct Words / ____ Total Words × 100 = ____% Words Correct

***Note:** For more information about how to calculate T-units, see pages 74–77 in the *Examiner's Manual*.

(continued)

Qualitative observations:

14+

WRITTEN EXPRESSION CONTENT UNITS SCORING FORM

Story D: "The Building" (p. 75)

1. There was a building.	0	1	18. People did not think about it.	0	1
2. It was old.	0	1	19. It was almost hidden.	0	1
3. No one knew how old.	0	1	20. They did not care.	0	1
4. There were no records.	0	1	21. Then something happened.	0	1
5. People talked about it.	0	1	22. The city wanted the land.	0	1
6. It had a history.	0	1	23. They needed a new road.	0	1
7. Some people knew.	0	1	24. The building would be demolished.	0	1
8. It was used in a war.	0	1	25. People suddenly cared.	0	1
9. It was long ago.	0	1	26. They wrote articles.	0	1
10. The building was a hospital.	0	1	27. They gave speeches.	0	1
11. Soldiers came there.	0	1	28. They raised money.	0	1
12. There were hundreds.	0	1	29. They saved the building.	0	1
13. Many were treated.	0	1	30. They saved the graveyard.*	0	1
14. Many died.	0	1	31. They saved something else.	0	1
15. They were buried.	0	1	32. It was their history.	0	1
16. The graveyard was still there.*	0	1	33. That was more important.	0	1
17. It was behind the building.	0	1		**Content Units total**	**/33**

*Note: Count graveyard as one word when counting total words for Written Expression regardless of spacing.

Discourse Score	____ Content Units / 33 possible × 100 = ____% Content Included
Sentence Score	____ Content Units / ____ T-units* = ____ Sentence Score (record 2 decimal places)
Word Score	____ Total Words − ____ Error Words = ____ Total Correct Words / ____ Total Words × 100 = ____% Words Correct

Note: For more information about how to calculate T-units, see pages 74–77 in the *Examiner's Manual.*

Qualitative observations:

SUBTEST 13: Social Communication (SC)

Average time to administer: 9 minutes

Materials: *Stimulus Book* (pp. 80–107 for boys; pp. 108–135 for girls), audio recording device (recommended)

Start rule: ➡ Start points for age ranges are indicated by arrows

Repetition: Allowed

Basal rule: 6 consecutive scores of 1

Ceiling rule: 6 scores of 0 out of 8 consecutive items

Directions

- Begin audio recording (recommended).
- Say, ***"This activity is about acting a scene, like from a show on TV or a movie. Your job is to be an actor."*** (Ask if the student ever watches movies, plays, or television shows and knows what an actor is.)
- Say, ***"I'll give you a really short scene. Then I'll ask you to tell me what one of the people would say. This is important—you should say it how the person would say it in the scene. Remember, you're the actor! Let's try one. I'll do the first one to show you."*** Administer practice item.

Probes If the student gives a one-word response, say, ***"Can you give me more?"***

Recording & Scoring

Record the student's response verbatim in the space provided.

- **Vocabulary score**
  Score 1 if the student conveys meaning of the key vocabulary [underlined] fitting the scene.
  Score 0 if the student does not capture the meaning.
- **Pragmatics score**
  Score 1 if the student communicates the social intent through appropriate phrasing and prosody for the social context (do not penalize shyness).
  Score 0 if the student does not convey the communicative intent with either phrasing or prosody.
- **Total Item score**
  Score 1 if the student earns a score of 1 on *both* parts.
  Score 0 if either part earns a 0.

Practice item for girls: ***"Jasmine always whines when her parents won't let her have her way. Her mother won't let her buy candy in the grocery store. What do you think Jasmine might say?"***

Practice item for boys: ***"Jarred always whines when his parents won't let him have his way. His mother won't let him buy candy in the grocery store. What do you think Jarred might say?"***

Give practice item response ***("Mom, I want some candy. Buy me some candy.")*** without tone, prosody, intensity, intonation, or gestures. Then say, ***"I could do it that way, but it's not very good acting. Here is how it sounds when I really try to talk like the person would in the scene."*** In an exaggerated whine, say, ***"Mom, I want some candy. Buy me some candy."*** Say, ***"Now you try it."*** Coach as necessary.

Then say, ***"Remember to be an actor! If you need me to repeat the information about the scene, I can."***
Say, ***"Any questions?"*** (Answer.) ***"Let's begin."***

Subtest Items

➡ 6–11

1. *(for girls)* **Sally's friend always brags about her dog. One day Sally decides to top her friend's bragging by telling how big her own dog is. What do you think Sally would say?**
1. *(for boys)* **Sam's friend always brags about his dog. One day Sam decides to top his friend's bragging by telling how big his own dog is. What do you think Sam would say?**

Student's response:	Vocabulary	Pragmatics	Item Score	
Brags about dog's size in a bragging tone.	1	1		
	0	0	0	1

2. *(for girls)* **Rita wants to argue with her friend about whose turn it is to go first playing a game. What do you think Rita would say?**
2. *(for boys)* **Rick wants to argue with his friend about whose turn it is to go first playing a game. What do you think Rick would say?**

Student's response:	Vocabulary	Pragmatics	Item Score	
Insists on taking a turn in an argumentative tone.	1	1		
	0	0	0	1

(continued)

12–14 3. *(for girls)* **Thelma disagrees with everything a friend says. Yesterday her friend suggested that they go to a movie on Friday. What do you think Thelma would say?**

3. *(for boys)* **Theo disagrees with everything a friend says. Yesterday his friend suggested that they go to a movie on Friday. What do you think Theo would say?**

Student's response:	Vocabulary	Pragmatics	Item Score	
Disagrees with plan for movie or going on Friday. May (or may not) suggest alternative.	1	1		
	0	0	0	1

4. *(for girls)* **Ms. Flynn always gets angry when her class doesn't listen. Her class is really noisy and Ms. Flynn decides to punish the class for not listening. What do you think Ms. Flynn would say?**

4. *(for boys)* **Mr. Flynn always gets angry when his class doesn't listen. His class is really noisy and Mr. Flynn decides to punish the class for not listening. What do you think Mr. Flynn would say?**

Student's response:	Vocabulary	Pragmatics	Item Score	
Uses teacher voice to tell students to quiet down (or some variation) and names a punishment.	1	1		
	0	0	0	1

5. *(for girls)* **Rachel wants to politely turn down an invitation to a party she thinks will be boring. What do you think Rachel would say?**

5. *(for boys)* **Ron wants to politely turn down an invitation to a party he thinks will be boring. What do you think Ron would say?**

Student's response:	Vocabulary	Pragmatics	Item Score	
Offers an excuse for not being able to attend in a polite tone, without saying anything about the party being boring.	1	1		
	0	0	0	1

15+ 6. *(for girls)* **Regina always bullies everyone. All of the kids want her to play soccer, but she will play only if they let her be the goalie. What do you think Regina would say?**

6. *(for boys)* **Reggie always bullies everyone. All of the kids want him to play soccer, but he will play only if they let him be the goalie. What do you think Reggie would say?**

Student's response:	Vocabulary	Pragmatics	Item Score	
Insists on being the goalie in a bullying tone.	1	1		
	0	0	0	1

7. *(for girls)* **Henry's big sister always orders him to do things for her. She wants him to wash her car. What do you think Henry's big sister would say?**

7. *(for boys)* **Holly's big brother always orders her to do things for him. He wants her to wash his car. What do you think Holly's big brother would say?**

Student's response:	Vocabulary	Pragmatics	Item Score	
Says "wash my car" (or some variation) in a tone that implies ordering. Does not say "please" or offer to pay.	1	1		
	0	0	0	1

(continued)

8. *(for girls)* **Ruth's mother always criticizes everything she does. When Ruth brings home her report card with two As and two Bs, what do you think her mother would say?**

8. *(for boys)* **Randy's father always criticizes everything he does. When Randy brings home his report card with two As and two Bs, what do you think his father would say?**

Student's response:	**Vocabulary**	**Pragmatics**	**Item Score**	
May praise the As, but must convey that the child could have done better.	1	1		
	0	0	0	1

9. *(for girls)* **Debby always uses hints to get her grandmother to buy her things. Debby is out shopping with her grandmother and sees some boots she wants. What do you think Debby would say?**

9. *(for boys)* **David always uses hints to get his grandmother to buy him things. David is out shopping with his grandmother and sees some boots he wants. What do you think David would say?**

Student's response:	**Vocabulary**	**Pragmatics**	**Item Score**	
Makes comments about how nice the boots are or needing boots but without asking for them directly. (Hinting about the color and shape or location of the boots does not score.)	1	1		
	0	0	0	1

10. *(for girls)* **The talk show host always flatters her guests. She is interviewing an actor. What do you think the talk show host would say?**

10. *(for boys)* **The talk show host always flatters his guests. He is interviewing an actor. What do you think the talk show host would say?**

Student's response:	**Vocabulary**	**Pragmatics**	**Item Score**	
Makes a flattering comment about the guest.	1	1		
	0	0	0	1

11. *(for girls)* **Sarita always encourages her friend to work on her running. Sarita's friend comes in second in a race. What do you think Sarita would say?**

11. *(for boys)* **Santos always encourages his friend to work on his running. Santos's friend comes in second in a race. What do you think Santos would say?**

Student's response:	**Vocabulary**	**Pragmatics**	**Item Score**	
Says something encouraging about continuing to work or coming close or makes a simple praise comment, such as "great job."	1	1		
	0	0	0	1

(continued)

12. *(for girls)* **Sheila always <u>fishes for compliments</u>. She was wearing her new clothes when she met her friend on the way to the school party. What do you think Sheila would say?**

12. *(for boys)* **Shawn always <u>fishes for compliments</u>. He was wearing his new clothes when he met his friend on the way to the school party. What do you think Shawn would say?**

Student's response:	**Vocabulary**	**Pragmatics**	**Item Score**	
Draws attention to self and/or clothes. May ask directly, "How do you like my new clothes?"	1	1		
	0	0	0	1

13. *(for girls)* **Nora always <u>sounds really sarcastic</u>. Let's say it rains every weekend all summer. What do you think Nora would say?**

13. *(for boys)* **Noah always <u>sounds really sarcastic</u>. Let's say it rains every weekend all summer. What do you think Noah would say?**

Student's response:	**Vocabulary**	**Pragmatics**	**Item Score**	
Says something ironic about liking all the rain using a sarcastic tone.	1	1		
	0	0	0	1

Total score: ______ / 13

Qualitative observations:

SUBTEST 14: Digit Span Forward (DSF)

Note: Subtest 14 can be used as a stand-alone measure or in conjunction with Subtest 15. If administered together with Subtest 15, Subtest 14 must be administered immediately before Subtest 15 and in the same session.

Average time to administer: 3 minutes

Materials: None

Start rule: ➡ Start points for age ranges are indicated by arrows

Repetition: No (unless ambient noise interferes)

Basal rule: Scores 1 on all items at any one level (a level is a set of items that all include the same number of digits and are shaded similarly)

Ceiling rule: Scores 0 on all items at any one level

Directions

- Say, ***"I am going to say some numbers. Listen to the numbers, and when I finish, you say them back to me exactly the same way."*** (*Note:* It is **important** to say the numbers at a rate of one per second in a neutral voice with even and equal stress.)
- ***"Here is one for practice: 4–2."*** If the student does not say "4–2," provide coaching and give this example: 8–6.
- Say, ***"Any questions?"*** (Answer.) ***"Let's begin."***

Probes

None

Recording & Scoring

- **Score 1** point for each correct sequence.
- **Score 0** for each incorrect sequence.
- **Score 0** for any unadministered items above the ceiling.
- Count the number of **1**s and enter as the total score.

Practice Items

Stimulus	Student's response
"4–2"	

Stimulus	Student's response
"8–6"	

Subtest Items

Start	Item	Stimulus	Student's response	Score	
6–8 ➡	1a.	"5–8–2"		0	1
	1b.	"4–1–8"		0	1
9+ ➡	2a.	"8–2–5–1"		0	1
	2b.	"6–4–9–3"		0	1
	3a.	"3–8–1–7–2"		0	1
	3b.	"7–5–1–4–9"		0	1
	4a.	"2–5–9–6–3–8"		0	1
	4b.	"9–2–5–8–1–4"		0	1
	4c.	"6–4–9–7–2–8"		0	1

Item	Stimulus	Student's response	Score	
5a.	"7–2–5–8–1–9–4"		0	1
5b.	"1–7–3–8–6–2–9"		0	1
5c.	"8–3–9–1–4–1–5"		0	1
6a.	"6–1–0–3–9–7–8–1"		0	1
6b.	"2–5–3–1–8–6–4–9"		0	1
6c.	"5–3–4–1–2–9–6–7"		0	1

Total score: ______ / 15

Qualitative observations:

SUBTEST 15: Digit Span Backward (DSB)

Note: Subtest 14 must be administered immediately prior to Subtest 15 and in the same session.

Average time to administer: 3 minutes
Materials: None
Start rule: ➡ Start points for age ranges are indicated by arrows
Repetition: No (unless ambient noise interferes)
Basal rule: Scores 1 on all items at any one level
Ceiling rule: Scores 0 on all items at any one level

Directions

- Say, ***"I am going to say some numbers again. Listen carefully like before, but this time, when I finish, you say them back to me in backward order."***
- ***"Here's one for practice. 4–2."*** If the student does not say "2–4," provide coaching and give the second example: 8–6.
- Say, ***"Here are the first test numbers. Are you ready?"*** Answer any questions before starting. Remember to present the numbers at the rate of one per second in a neutral voice with equal and even stress. Give Part a and Part b, and/or Part c of each item before moving to the next item.

Probes
None

Recording & Scoring

- **Score 1** point for each correct reverse sequence.
- **Score 0** for each incorrect reverse sequence.
- **Score 0** for any unadministered items above the ceiling.
- Count the number of **1**s and enter as the total score.

Practice Items

Stimulus	Student's response
"4–2"	______ (2–4)
"8–6"	______ (6–8)

Subtest Items

Start	Item	Stimulus	Student's response	Score	
6–14 ➡	1a.	"5–8–2"	______ (2–8–5)	0	1
	1b.	"4–1–8"	______ (8–1–4)	0	1
	1c.	"9–3–7"	______ (7–3–9)	0	1
15+ ➡	2a.	"6–4–9–3"	______ (3–9–4–6)	0	1
	2b.	"8–2–5–1"	______ (1–5–2–8)	0	1
	2c.	"7–3–1–9"	______ (9–1–3–7)	0	1
	3a.	"3–8–1–7–2"	______ (2–7–1–8–3)	0	1
	3b.	"7–5–1–4–9"	______ (9–4–1–5–7)	0	1
	3c.	"2–9–7–4–8"	______ (8–4–7–9–2)	0	1
	4a.	"2–5–9–6–3–8"	______ (8–3–6–9–5–2)	0	1
	4b.	"9–2–5–8–1–4"	______ (4–1–8–5–2–9)	0	1
	4c.	"6–1–3–2–7–9"	______ (9–7–2–3–1–6)	0	1
	5a.	"7–2–5–8–1–9–4"	______ (4–9–1–8–5–2–7)	0	1
	5b.	"1–7–3–8–6–2–9"	______ (9–2–6–8–3–7–1)	0	1
	5c.	"3–8–1–6–7–2–5"	______ (5–2–7–6–1–8–3)	0	1

Total score: ______ **/ 15**

Qualitative observations:

[THIS PAGE LEFT INTENTIONALLY BLANK]

Identification Chart

Purpose: **To identify language and literacy disorders**

Step 1: Enter the Sum of the Subtest Standard Scores from the age-appropriate column for the Identification Core Score section from the Scoring Chart on the front cover of this *Examiner Record Form.*

Step 2: Compare this score to the appropriate age band and cut score. Check the decision box to the right of the table.

Age Band	Sum of Identification Core Standard Scores	Cut Score	Sensitivity	Specificity
6–7 years		24	84	84
8–11 years		34	88	85
12–18 years		42	86	90

Decision:
Is the Identification Core composite less than the cut score?

❒ Yes
This score is consistent with the presence of a language/literacy disorder.

❒ No
This score is not consistent with the presence of a language/literacy disorder.

Note: The confidence in the diagnostic decision is related to the sensitivity and specificity values for the student's age. Please refer to Chapter 2 of the *Technical Manual* for more information. Be sure to use the *Sum* of the Identification Core Standard Scores and *not* the Standard Score of the Identification Core Composite for comparison to the cut score.

Tracking Chart

Purpose: **To track changes in language and literacy skills over time**

Step 1: Enter the Standard Score obtained at Test Time 1 (from an earlier administration of the TILLS) and Test Time 2 (from the current administration) for each subtest administered.

Step 2: Subtract standard scores earned at Time 1 from scores earned at Time 2 to calculate differences.

Step 3: Compare the absolute values of the differences (i.e., ignoring whether they are positive or negative) to the True Change Interval values. (These represent values for the 68% confidence interval; values for the 90% confidence interval are reported in the Appendix of the *Examiner's Manual.*)

Step 4: If the absolute value of the difference for a subtest is larger than the True Change Interval, enter "yes" (or Y) under Change Decision. If not, enter "no" (or N). If yes, add a sign (+ or –) to indicate whether the difference is positive or negative.

DATE OF TEST	AGE OF STUDENT
Test Time 2: ________	______ yrs ______ mos
Test Time 1: ________	______ yrs ______ mos
Time between tests: ____________	*(minimum 6 months)*

	Oral Language						Written Language					
	Sub-test	Standard Score Time 2	Standard Score Time 1	Difference	True Change Interval	Change Decision (yes/no)	Sub-test	Standard Score Time 2	Standard Score Time 1	Difference	True Change Interval	Change Decision (yes/no)
Sound/Word Level	PA				2		NW Read				1	
Sound/Word Level	NW Rep				2		RF				2	
Sound/Word Level	DSF				2		NW Spell				1	
Sound/Word Level	DSB				2		WE-Word				2	
Sent/Disc Level	VA				1		RC				2	
Sent/Disc Level	LC				2		WE-Disc				1	
Sent/Disc Level	FD				2		WE-Sent				1	
Sent/Disc Level	SR				2							
Sent/Disc Level	DSR				2							
Sent/Disc Level	SC				2							

Key: PA = Phonemic Awareness, NWRep = Nonword Repetition, DSF = Digit Span Forward, DSB = Digit Span Backward, VA = Vocabulary Awareness, LC = Listening Comprehension, FD = Following Directions, SR = Story Retelling, DSR = Delayed Story Retelling, SC = Social Communication, NWRead = Nonword Reading, RF = Reading Fluency, NWSpell = Nonword Spelling, WE-Word = Written Expression–Word Score, RC = Reading Comprehension, WE-Disc = Written Expression–Discourse Score, WE-Sent = Written Expression–Sentence Score

Profile Chart

Purpose: To document patterns of relative strengths and weaknesses

The Profile Chart re-orders the subtests of the TILLS model so that the scores portray a performance profile for the student; take care to enter the scores correctly.

Step 1: For each subtest administered, enter the Standard Score from the Scoring Chart (on the front cover) in the white cell at the top of the corresponding subtest column in the Profile Chart.

Step 2: Mark an X over the dot for the corresponding score in the column.

Step 3: Draw a vertical line from the X to the horizontal line representing the mean in the chart (at standard score 10).

		Oral Language										Written Language						
		Sound/Word Level				Sentence/Discourse Level						Sound/Word Level				Sent/Disc Level		
		PA	NW Rep	DSF	DSB	VA	LC	FD	SR	DSR	SC	NW Read	RF	NW Spell	WE-Word	RC	WE-Disc	WE-Sent
	Standard Score																	
+2 SD	16–19	•	•	•	•	•	•	•	•	•	•	•	•	•	•	•	•	•
	15	•	•	•	•	•	•	•	•	•	•	•	•	•	•	•	•	•
	14	•	•	•	•	•	•	•	•	•	•	•	•	•	•	•	•	•
+1 SD	13	•	•	•	•	•	•	•	•	•	•	•	•	•	•	•	•	•
	12	•	•	•	•	•	•	•	•	•	•	•	•	•	•	•	•	•
	11	•	•	•	•	•	•	•	•	•	•	•	•	•	•	•	•	•
Mean	10	•	•	•	•	•	•	•	•	•	•	•	•	•	•	•	•	•
	9	•	•	•	•	•	•	•	•	•	•	•	•	•	•	•	•	•
	8	•	•	•	•	•	•	•	•	•	•	•	•	•	•	•	•	•
−1 SD	7	•	•	•	•	•	•	•	•	•	•	•	•	•	•	•	•	•
	6	•	•	•	•	•	•	•	•	•	•	•	•	•	•	•	•	•
	5	•	•	•	•	•	•	•	•	•	•	•	•	•	•	•	•	•
−2 SD	4	•	•	•	•	•	•	•	•	•	•	•	•	•	•	•	•	•
	3	•	•	•	•	•	•	•	•	•	•	•	•	•	•	•	•	•
	2	•	•	•	•	•	•	•	•	•	•	•	•	•	•	•	•	•
−3 SD	1	•	•	•	•	•	•	•	•	•	•	•	•	•	•	•	•	•
↓	0	•	•	•	•	•	•	•	•	•	•	•	•	•	•	•	•	•

Confidence Intervals (CI)

	PA	NW Rep	DSF	DSB	VA	LC	FD	SR	DSR	SC	NW Read	RF	NW Spell	WE-Word	RC	WE-Disc	WE-Sent
Upper CI value (+) for __% level																	
Standard Score																	
Lower CI value (-) for __% level																	

Step 4: In the table above, fill in the student's Standard Score for each subtest administered.

Step 5: Decide whether to use the 68% or the 90% confidence interval; write in the one selected. Look up the corresponding CI values for the student's age in the Appendix in the *Examiner's Manual.*

Step 6: Add and subtract these values from each Standard Score, and enter the resulting numbers in the appropriate upper and lower confidence interval value boxes.

Step 7: In the Profile Chart above, draw short horizontal lines through the dots corresponding to the upper and lower CI boundaries.

	TILLS Total	Sound/Word Composite	Sent/Disc Composite	Oral Composite	Written Composite	Identification Core
Upper CI value (+) for __% level						
Standard Score						
Lower CI value (-) for __% level						

ISBN-13: 978-1-59857-830-0
ISBN-10: 1-59857-830-8

· P A U L · H ·
BROOKES
PUBLISHING Co.®
www.brookespublishing.com

Test of Integrated Language and Literacy Skills™ (TILLS™)
by Nickola Wolf Nelson, Ph.D., Elena Plante, Ph.D.,
Nancy Helm-Estabrooks, Sc.D., and Gillian Hotz, Ph.D.

Printed in the United States of America.

9 781598 578300 90000